I WANT TO SMACK MY BOSS

Exploring the Dynamics of a Multi-Generational Workforce

by

Denise-Danielle

I Want to Smack My Boss: Exploring the Dynamics of A Multi-Generational Workforce
Denise-Danielle
ISBN: 9781522048572
© 2017. All rights reserved. No part of this publication may be reproduced, distributed, or
transmitted in any form or by any means, including photocopying, recording, or other electronic
or mechanical methods, without the prior written permission of the publisher, except in the case
of brief quotations embodied in critical reviews and certain other noncommercial uses permitted by copyright law

Table of Contents

Introduction 3
Opinion 1 10
   Millennials Are Not the Only Generation @ Work 10
Opinion 2 23
   Information Is Different from Wisdom 23
Opinion 3 37
   Not Everyone Understands Leadership 37
Opinion 4 52
   Management Skills Are Not Gained Through Promotion 52
Opinion 5 67
   Commitment Has Changed Its Look 67
Opinion 6 74
   Hidden Issues Cause Damage 74
Opinion 7 93
   Learning the Art of Shut Up 93
A Personal Note 106
References 108

INTRODUCTION

Is the workplace today a great masterpiece we have perfected over the decades or merely a paint-by-numbers project, and we are constantly trying to fix the places where we have painted outside the lines?

Over the last twenty years technology, cultural changes, and various events have impacted how we live, work, and socialize with one another. Indeed, we have made significant advances in the workplace through technology, a more connected global market, improved methods to share information, improved communication systems, and much more. In fact, these advances have been so impactful they have created opportunities for small and mid-size organizations. The playing field of the business world has been leveled, and anyone can play and be successful. But being a player requires agility, innovation, the ability to shift from the past, and a balanced approach to business management. Regardless, of an organization's size, the core components of an organization remain the same. In my opinion, business is the intersection of people, money, and resources. "People" include anyone impacted by an organization product or service directly or indirectly, financially, mentally, or emotionally. "Money" relates to all resources that can be used for financing, including cash, stocks, credit, and assets, real estate or otherwise. Essentially, anything that can be leveraged to expand market position. "Resources" can include anything that supports production or delivery of products and services, such as buildings, technology, and materials. If these three areas are not properly managed, they can impact the success of any organization, no matter the size.

The "people" of this equation include shareholders, board of directors, employees, suppliers, customers, and the media. Companies are investing millions to remain at the very top and keep many of these groups happy by delivering consistent profits, innovations, and expansion in the marketplace. However, one essential element been overlooked in this equation! Properly managing the workforce of employees is as essential.

Today's workforce is diverse and unique compared to previous generations, a collage of various generations, experiences, backgrounds, and career paths. Degrees of differences between work ethics, work experience, and expectations of how to operate and interact in the workplace (workplace social diplomacy) exist. Unfortunately, these differences are not creating beautiful masterpieces but rather frustrations, anxieties, fears, low morale, and anger.

The professional workplace consists of a collage of people who entered the workforce in the last decade and workers whose careers span back to before the use of many technologies integral to the modern workplace, such as email, fax machines, instant messaging, or text messages. New workers may be excited to be embarking on the initial steps of their career paths while others envision themselves at different levels of success or perhaps retired. Despite planning and diligence the current financial crisis, unforeseen changes in global markets, and the expansion of technology have had a significant impact on many lives and career paths.

These changes outside of the workplace have caused shifts forcing individuals to take on new roles and responsibilities. Roles have become obsolete, causing workers to search for new job openings, develop new skill sets, or take on subordinate or higher positions. The marketplace cries out and demands faster returns, more innovation, and more ability to relate to a global and diverse marketplace. Organizations find themselves pushed to respond to the market or risk the chance of becoming obsolete in a fast moving and ever changing and demanding environment. The workforce is pushed to move and respond as quickly as possible or suffer the consequence of being absent from the future. Workers who can address immediate needs are promoted quickly but at what cost?

This new dynamic gives birth to some unique opportunities in the workplace to expand into new markets, build new skills, and experience working with a global workforce. On the other hand, these changes may also raise issues that cause an uncomfortable or a stressful working environment, causing many to think, "I Want to Smack my Boss."

The idea for this book came to me a few years ago on a return flight from a business trip. I was tired, and the traveling airline had not yet caught up with the idea of in-flight entertainment. So as I gazed out at a dark sky, my mind began replaying the events of a tedious week on a client project. One of my teammates had come to the company to help develop a training program but seemed to run into issues with project management. She was a seasoned training developer and had done all sorts of work in this particular field. She came to the company because she wanted to work on projects where she lived and was going through some personal life changing events. Her only daughter was about to give birth to her first grandchild, and she wanted to stay in the area. She continued to run into encounters with managers who neither understand training nor had experience in this field, but wanted to tell her how to do the job since they were in a leadership role. Consequently, she found herself micromanaged and later became frustrated and eventually left the company. It was a situation where individuals had been placed in manager level roles but lacked the skills for managing a seasoned workforce.

As I pondered this event, similar stories, conversations, and personal experiences began to flood my mind. I recalled receiving a call from a hiring manager who wanted to get my thoughts on a potential hire for a high-tech company in California looking to launch some marketing campaigns using the internet and social media tools. They were looking for an employee who understood this environment and could help develop content. The conversation went well, and just before we hung up, the hiring manager had one last question that I thought was interesting. Despite all the other positive information I gave she wanted to know if the individual we had discussed would show up for work on time consistently and demonstrate a good work ethic. After addressing her concerns, I was curious to know the reason behind the question. Apparently the hiring manager had experienced the event of younger staff who stopped showing up for work without any sort of notice, no call, no email, not even a text message. This poor work ethic was affecting the organization and was a major concern and consideration for hiring. An expectation of quickly advancing up the corporate ladder seemed to exist among some younger workers, but the accompanying desire to put in the years of experience was absent. So, in essence, she had a need for a particular skill set, but the workers who tended to fit that profile had a problem with commitment. I might argue that this is nothing new in the workplace. However, this dynamic seems to be showing up a lot more in recent years than in other generations of workforces.

We could say this is just a problem with the workforce, but I have learned every situation has two sides. Despite age or years of experience, younger generations are growing up in organizations that groom them as future leaders and want them to move up the ladder quickly. This rapid ascent, for a person with less than ten years of professional experience to manage or lead a team versus an individual with over twenty or thirty years of work experience, is neither uncommon nor unusual. The problem is not with the age of the manager but their level of experience. A person may have a particular skill set but lack the experience or wisdom to provide a broader understanding of the situation to manage a seasoned workforce. Consequently, the entire weight of problem solving may fall on the shoulders of the seasoned employee. On the contrary, we are also seeing more seasoned employees who lead teams of individuals with five years or less of professional work experience. The experienced employees have the experience but may resist change or the adoption of new ideas, procedures, and technology. They are stuck in the past while the rest of the world is charging ahead aggressively. This situation can cause a team or organization to fall behind competitors and find it tough to catch up in the future. Many stories like these, in addition to my personal experience, have been instrumental in shaping a few opinions I have developed on this subject about the impact I believe this dynamic is having on the workforce and workplace. This book is my attempt to bring the problem into the light.

"If you are going to write a book, have an opinion because there are enough books on the market with just information," said my brother Sidney. In this book I share some of my opinions based on what I have seen going on in today's workforce and how it is impacting the work environment, hindering creativity, and possibly stifling one of the greatest moments of history. Imagine what could be created if we understood how to build environments where multiple generations collaborate and design solutions that impact today, tomorrow, and future generations.

OPINION 1

Millennials Are Not the Only Generation @ Work

Obviously the workforce today consists of more than one generation. Many of us may have gotten this revelation, heard a speaker talk about the multi-generational labor force, read a blog, or news article. Despite all this revelation about this multi-generational workforce, the only planning organizations and businesses seem to make centers around one group: Millennials. The Millennial generation is defined as young adults from ages 13 to 32; born 1980–1999.[1] How we work, how we communicate, and how we manage business seems to be driven by how this one group reacts and wants to be treated.

The rationale I hear is that this group is the largest generation since the Baby Boomers, and like the Baby Boomers, Millennials seem to be influencing everything, whether that is a new product launch, how a workforce is managed, or how we live and communicate with one another.[1] Whether or not this spending power is realistic can be debated. If I go to work, receive my paycheck, and subsequently use these funds to make purchases, I have used my spending power. However, if the source of these funds that I used to make these purchases is someone other than myself (parent or grand-parent), then I am not the true spender in this scenario. It would seem we are stretching to say one group has considerable spending power when their paychecks are not the source of the funds being spent. We appear to be trying to drive an argument in which the control of the resources and an official source of the funds are not the purchaser. In other words, if I don't control the funds, I don't have the power over how those funds are used. I may have an influence, but my power to control is limited to the other persons (resource holders) and their willingness to yield. The one who holds the money has the real power.

Economic hardships have been hitting harder in the last fifteen years, which has impacted the ability of young people to grow financially independent because they have become shackled to high levels of debt. Younger generations have had to learn how to rely on parents or grandparents to survive and obtain even the most basic needs, such as housing.[2] Consequently, if other generations are the ones able to maintain the resources, we had better figure out how to keep them employed. In reality, the older generation supporting the unemployed or underemployed young, indebted generation is playing a significant role in real spending power. Ignoring this fact builds a foundation that is neither accurate nor stable, thus impacting all of our futures.

Looking at the data and acknowledging what we truly see versus making up what we desire to see is important. In the United States, we have a history of looking at data and extracting what we want to see and ignoring the rest. Unfortunately, the consequences of this practice have been economic failures such as a few dot.com companies in Silicon Valley late 90's and early 2000 and the blow up of the real estate bubble in 2007. In both cases the truth was evident, yet decisions made focused on making money, ignoring the truth of the situation. In a global economy, mistakes made in one nation are no longer isolated but have the potential to impact the world's economic structure.

Signs we should think about include the real source of the finances to make purchases; in other words: the one who is providing the cash to buy products and services. The real estate financial crash taught that credit is not cash because if the credit goes unpaid, the problem simply shifts to another victim. The potential to cause severe financial crisis in the larger picture because cash flow problems are not solved through credit is only exacerbated by delay.

Our society has become very sophisticated with technology, credit, tailored financial instruments, and method of financial exchange for goods and services. However, at the end of the day, accounting and finances are simple and dealt with in the same light as they have been for generations: exchanging something of value from one party to obtain goods or services from another party. Credit will never be a sustaining source of growth for any expanding society because mentally one remains disconnected thus can easily walk away. In a nutshell, the source of the valued object, whether cash, stocks, or property and regardless of the age of the spender, is the source of the buying power. Keeping everyone working and collecting a paycheck benefits society.

Generational bickering overshadows debate of the real problems. The person who holds the money holds the power. When I work, I get a paycheck and have buying power. If I don't work, I am a dependent and must rely on others to provide for my needs, and I am a slave to their power. If I borrow, I am a slave to the lender and subject to the lender's terms and conditions. If I am unable to sustain my lifestyle without assistance for long periods of time then I don't have true buying power. I may have influence, but I do not have buying power: the idea of any true power is an illusion that will quickly disappear the moment a financial storm arises.

So the question that arises is where are the jobs? A report by the World Economic Forum states, "...disruptive changes to business models will have a profound impact on the employment landscape over the coming years." Organizations are outsourcing many transactional and entry level positions, and we are stepping into the initial stages of the Fourth Industrial Revolution. A change in skill sets will accompany this transition, including overall social skills, and a shifting into new skills, such as understanding data analytics and ability to work with new technology, will be pertinent.[4] Indeed, the power of influence is important and should not be ignored, but always consider the depth of this power and the extent and degree of influence.

Millennials have driven the use of social media to communicate and stay connected. Their ability to purchase and influence others has driven the development of new technologies. In fact, this group has led the way in how we use and leverage social media to stay connected. As a group, the fact they spend more hours during the day staying connected to media sites has influenced the behaviors of many organizations. Organizations that originally shunned the idea of social media have now adapted and driven their company objectives to improve social media presence and interactions with customers. The use of social media has established a platform for purchasers to interact with one another, provide feedback on product services, and drive improvements through the customer experience. Consumers are now empowered with tools to get their voices heard to such a degree that larger organizations have started to pay attention.[1]

Social media has expanded the platforms to share ideas and helped connect a global world, increasing collaboration across organizations and diverse cultures. Social media has empowered small voices to become much louder and influential and created a platform for an individual to launch a small and profitable business in a short period of time through the development of apps (applications). As the Millennial generation has taken the lead in adopting these tools, they have helped all generations experience new levels of creativity and connectivity. On the other hand, this innovation has also raised social issues in the workplace that did not exist in previous generations. Older generations have neglected to share knowledge that has been transferred through generations about discretion. In the past, workers clearly understood what information should be shared broadly and what information should be shared only amongst family and close friends or small groups. The line between personal life and workplace life has gotten blurred over the past two decades for many, and people now have a difficult time identifying the boundaries. Information once considered personal and unsuitable for the workplace is now shared across social media, at the water cooler, in break rooms, and even at meetings.

During my college days, I participated in a cooperative work program. As part of the program, it was mandatory to attend a business etiquette course that addressed how to eat at business dinners, the best food to order during a lunch meeting, resume presentation, appropriate business dress, and methods of presenting yourself in a professional manner at all times. During my professional career, I also had mentors who would pull me to the side and instruct me on the intricacies of office etiquette. I was taught to understand that I was not only representing myself but the company, and therefore I needed to act and present myself accordingly. This philosophy is considered old school, and perhaps this tact is less accepting of the individual and the uniqueness an individual brings to an organization. It was not intended to hinder uniqueness but maintain the uniqueness of the organization.

Before sharing information, an individual should ponder who will view content; family and friends tend to be more forgiving and forgetful than coworkers or employers. Consider what gets posted to social media sites and the audience who will be reading any given post. Also, consider the fact that anything posted can be shared to an audience much broader than an immediate circle. I have seen coworkers get upset, frustrated, and burned out by something that happened at work and post a derogatory comment on a social media site. Unfortunately, this moment of frustration lives much longer than the anger that spawned it, and sometimes the comment is noted by other work colleagues who are less forgiving, including upper management.

Overall, I am not against posting thoughts or sharing information on social media, but a level of discretion should be executed. Some people are like Niagara Falls, and information just flows out of their mouths with no sense of a filter. If your personal information is at the top of their thoughts, chances are your personal information will come flowing out with everything else. If you are not prepared to endure the consequences of posting personal information, then execute discretion.

In addition to social media changing the way business is done today and how we interact and collaborate, changes are taking place in how and where work is done. Organizations are becoming more comfortable with remote workforces and altering the methods and frequency in which on-the-job training is performed. In the past, working from home was considered unique, but in some industries, such as technology consulting it has become a common practice. Organizations can reduce the cost of owning and managing real estate and also be able to have a more flexible workforce if workers work from home. Employees can have a better balance between work and life, which has become more and more of a benefit for current workforce.[3]

Although much positive press and conversation about all the changes in the workplace driven by the Millennials exists, the negatives, such as depression, lack of commitment, and high debt, should not be ignored. According to popular opinion, Millennials are also likely to walk off of a job more quickly than their predecessors. Additionally, a prevailing thought that a majority of Baby Boomers are tired of working and are ready to head out the workplace door to retirement also exists. However, during a casual conversation with Baby Boomers, I, at least, don't get the impression there will be this mass exodus of this entire generation. It is the case that some are looking forward to a change and dream about the sailboat of retirement shortly, but others like working and don't see themselves retiring anytime soon. For some the very thought of retirement is frightening. A generation who has experienced everything from manual typewriters to texting is excited about the opportunities to participate in the great transformation into the new age of technology. They have been involved in wars and overcome some deplorable acts of inhumanity. They are not a generation in general to sit on the sidelines.

So here is the big picture: at one end are the Millennials, who are perceived to be entering the workforce door with high expectations and demands, high debt, depression, and lack commitment, and at the other end, are the Baby Boomers, who are perceived to be inflexible and headed out the door for retirement. In the middle, you have a bunch of other generations; that hardly ever gets mentioned whose influences and contributions seem meager when compared to the other two groups.

I am not an economist, but the way I interpret this big picture is; Houston, we have a problem. Yes, this younger generation has surpassed the Baby Boomers in size and has a perceived purchase power and influence beyond its actual reach. And, a lot of expectation has been placed on their shoulders. However, have we also thought about the fact that they have debt, depression, and a lack of commitment to work? From where does a Millennial's money actually flow, and what happens when they continue to borrow money with such high debt? To where do they return if they can't pay the rent or mortgage? Who really drives purchasing power? Could it be the Baby Boomers or those other generations who never get mentioned, but somehow responsible for holding up the middle? Remember, debt is not purchasing power but merely the delay of payment.

I am sure there is a portion of people from various older generations who would love to retire and kick back to enjoy the good life but can't because their once empty nest is filled with their Millennial children. Therefore, despite popular demand and the lack of appreciation at the office, they have no choice but to continue to press on and allow the sailboat of retirement to wait a little longer.

Each generation has been given unique God-given gifts and the responsibility to share and support one another. Yes, some generations are larger than others, but that does not negate importance or ability to contribute. We need the innovative nature of the Millennials and the passion to drive for change, but we also need the consistency, drive, and wisdom of the Baby Boomers and older generations, and all the gifts and talents of the in-between generation to teach how to support and bridge gaps.

Economists and others have been predicting the retirement and impact of the Baby Boomer generation for years and have gotten it wrong. In fact, many thought they would be retiring, but the harsh realities of economic crashes have changed those plans. During my brief stint as a financial advisor, I recall the various conversations with people who saw their dreams vanish. Heads low and voices soft they would recount how retirement accounts and plans had faded, as if it were something that was stolen in the middle of the night.

I don't see the workforce or the economy going the way people are predicting. In fact, I see our economy getting worse, and more people suffering mentally, financially, spiritually, and physically. I see problems increasing in the workplace and flowing over into homes, communities, cities, and states. I see people carrying more stress because they are carrying homes, debt, and lifestyles of others on their shoulders.

World Economic Forum on Jobs stated, "A number of promising approaches appear underutilized across almost all industries. For example, a focus on making better use of the accumulated experiences of older employees and building an ageless workforce barely registers among proposed workforce strategies."[4] Humanity as a whole is no stranger to challenges, but we have learned to band together to face and overcome challenges. The challenges of the future will initially look different and seem unconquerable, but if we learn to band together, when we look back on these days, we may yet see another victory.

Seppanen, S.S., and W. Gualtieri. National Chamber Foundation. 2012. *The Millennial Generation Research Review.*
² Pew Research Center. March 7, 2014. *Millennials in Adulthood, Detached from Institutions, Networked with Friends.*
³ Deloitte 2016 Millennial Survey. *Winning over the next Generation of Leaders.*
⁴ World Economic Forum Report. 2016. *Future of Jobs.*

OPINION 2

Information Is Different from Wisdom

Data constantly bombard us, feeding us constant streams of information on various topics from Hollywood gossip and the latest fashions to current events and political opinions. In addition to our personal devices, electronic billboards fill our streets delivering rotating messages along roads, buses, and public areas. The moment I open my eyes to the last minute of the day, my eyes and ears are constantly bombarded with almost unfiltered information. In today's culture 140 characters coming quick in small bite sizes give digestible knowledge. The current perception is the quicker and more digestible, the more informative, and the more a person consumes of this data, the smarter a person becomes.

Have you ever overheard a conversation in public? Periodically, I will sit and listen to conversations taking place around me. I am astounded by the number of people who seem to be an authority on any given subject matter who cross my path each day. However, as I continue to listen, I find it fascinating how many people regurgitate information they have heard or read as if they were the author and an authority on any given subject. They have read a few articles, books, blog entries, or tweets, or maybe they have only seen something on Facebook, and now are a storehouse of information. They are now prepared to share this vast wealth of knowledge and insight.

Imagine holding a conversation with one of these storehouses of information. They stand tall, and confidently with passion and authority, quote verbatim all of the books they have read. I have learned to stop and ask if the person to whom I am listening is transferring knowledge or if they have obtained actual wisdom on the subject.

It's not a matter of judging someone for sharing information, but merely a method of managing my level of expectations and establishing how much value to place on the conversation. Also if I need information, then just regurgitated facts are fine, but if I am looking for true wisdom on a particular subject, this person may not be who I need to be talking to. We must understand reading a book, and other sources of information are good, and they are great resources for acquiring knowledge, gaining clarity, and getting a greater understanding of a subject. However, the act of gathering textbook knowledge and repacking it or adding a fancy title is not wisdom but a transfer of information.

I am a big fan of the Italian dessert, cannoli, but I am very specific about where and whose I eat. If I happen to be in an Italian restaurant, I will usually see if cannoli is on the menu, but before ordering, I ask the server a few questions. First, I want to know if the cannoli is made fresh on the premises then I ask about the ingredients. If at any point in this process, the server stalls or gives a rehearsed answer, I know the dessert is probably not made on the premises but frozen, and the ingredients may not be fresh. The restaurant is performing the role of connecting buyer to manufacturer, so consequently they only know as much information as they the manufacturer has provided, which means they can only be in a position to transfer knowledge.

However, when I visit my hometown city of Philadelphia, there is a particular Italian bakery (Varallo Brothers) I frequent that makes some of the best cannoli I have ever tasted. Anyone in the bakery can reel off the ingredients without thought and can answer any other questions regarding the baking. They didn't read the packaged ingredients but have spent years and generations perfecting this product; they have wisdom about the cannoli. Needless to say, a person can taste the experience in the product, and it is marvelous.

The very essence of wisdom is an experience. Experience means I have gotten intimate with the subject, soiled and dirty with the subject by putting my hands into it and working with it for a period of time. It means I have done something so much or have such familiarity, that my subject and I are one. I have grown into the experience, and it has become a part of my DNA. No longer can one be separate from the other.

For instance, once during a trip to Panama, while scouting the countryside for a concert, I decided to take a little break and go for a drive to see a few new home developments in the area. As I drove one of the backcountry roads, I made a quick stop at a local farm stand. A member of our party, a native of Panama, suggested I try one of the locally grown bananas. The banana I ate was fresh from the tree, creamier and smoother than those I had eaten in the United States. This Panama banana saturated my mouth with flavor, and my taste buds danced with delight. I inquired as to why the huge difference in taste. My associate told me, it is because they leave the bananas on the tree vines until full maturity, thus gaining nutrients and flavor. The banana remained in position long enough to allow the nutrients to become part of its DNA, which in turn influenced its taste.

On the outside, a Panama banana looked the same as any other banana. It was not until I took a bite, made it a part of me and became intimate with it that I noticed those intricate, subtle creamy smooth differences. Overall, I did not realize how accustomed to the taste of my local bananas I had become until those Panamanian delights awakened my taste buds.

Two things to note: the bananas in Panama tastes different because they are given time to mature and gain experience or, in this case, flavor. Secondly, my eyes were opened because I stepped away from my usual routine and tried something different. In the end, I left satisfied having had the experience in Panama, but a little disappointed because now my American bananas would never taste the same. If before my visit to Panama, I had come across an article regarding the taste of these bananas, I would have gained more knowledge and information about the product, but I still would not have understood the difference between the tastes of bananas I eat in the United States versus the one I ate in Panama. If the article even happened to mention the taste, I still only would have information to share with others not real experience. If I happened to come across this article after my travels and my experience of tasting these bananas, I not only have information from the article, but I also have my personal experience that allows me to understand at an entirely different level. At that point, the information obtained from reading merely supports my wisdom obtained through the experience. If I happen to come into contact with someone who has read multiple articles but never tasted a banana from Panama, my experience will trump all of their information and knowledge obtained from reading. Indeed, they may have more information about the taste, but I have the experience of the taste. I can read the same articles and gain the knowledge and understanding as my friend, which bundled with my experience, will always place me at an advantage.

I draw lots of parallels between food and wisdom because they seem to have similar characteristics. When I eat, no one looks at me and identifies what part of my body consists of the apple, the steak, the fish, or the carrots. Once each element is digested, they all become a part of my body, my blood, and the essence of what makes up the whole of who I am and how I function. My wisdom is a culmination of all of my experiences and part of how I act, react, think, and execute. When I joined consulting and began doing journey and change management I was an oddball and stood out like a sore thumb. Many of the other practitioners were used to following a process approach to change management, but I looked at everything differently. I wanted to paint outside the process and push for more customized approaches. I understand process works well when delivering a large scale message that everyone, regardless of their experiences, needs to execute and deliver. At the time I had the habit of looking at everything through different sets of lenses. My father owned his own business, and I recall the experience of dealing with employees, finances, a budget, and resource management. Also, I spent a number of years in public accounting as an auditor and a few years in pharmaceutical sales, so even though I was in a role as a change lead, I automatically stepped back to look at the big picture and see how everything tied together. In my mind change management was less about moving people along a change curve, creating communication plans, developing training materials, and leadership development and more about selling people on a future vision and gaining their buy-in whether good or bad and all the other items (communication plan, training, coaching, leadership development) were tools to help get them to the commitment.

Initially, people would ask why I was making a certain decision, and I honestly did not know. I had no clue that my experiences were driving my actions or choices, and the wisdom I had was a culmination of these past experiences. All I knew was that certain things seemed to make sense. On one project I worked on, the vice president of the company had just been placed over a department that was being transformed. During the initial stages of the relationship, the team members were unhappy, challenged all recommendations, and nit-picked how everything was done. The leader on the project was so focused on the change management process and deliverables that they never looked up or listened to what the client was saying. The client had problems articulating the real needs and focused on pointing out problems and verbalizing overall disappointment. However, after the leader rolled off of the project, I ended up taking over the project and making a few changes in the focus. Listening to the concerns of the client helped me to understand that the client's concern was image and how the new department would be perceived by the larger organization. Consequently, we made adjustments to how things were communicated and the look and feel of communications and launched other key initiatives to improve department image. The result was a happy, satisfied client.

Wisdom has less to do with age and research and more about an experience. In a life-threatening situation, you would be better off listening to someone who has been in a similar situation and survived rather than someone with just information on how to survive. The workplace in the last decade has changed tremendously and continues to change on a daily basis. Technology, a more connected global market, and the advancement of other cultures and nations continue to add pressure to the business world. As these changes arise gaining the experience once common in the workforce seems impossible, so that lack of experience is rationalized away. A competent workforce must be able to identify changes and make those changes quickly to survive in a fast paced global market. Today's workforce must learn to adapt to a rapidly changing market. However, this gives an even greater reason for the need for real wisdom in the workplace and not just people with information.

Perhaps, we are looking through old lenses and telling ourselves that people with information or knowledge are truly wise. In reality, true wisdom has been absent from the workforce for so long that its true character is unrecognizable. Today, we see people who read multiple books on a subject. They will write a book with a nice new title, and they will be called subject matter experts and considered an authority on a particular area or topic. Many in our current workforce can articulate thoughts well and use big words that sound incredibly intelligent yet lack an understanding of a project or the assignment at hand. This practice clouds judgment and may impede the ability to lead others through a situation. To be honest, I do not have a problem with people who read and share it with others. These people do very well as long as the problem follows a prescribed pattern or process flow that follows an ideal business model. What happens when an issue in the workplace arises and does not follow a prescribed pattern, but takes a shift in another direction? Workplace problems, for the most part, do not follow textbook scenarios. In fact, in the next few years, I believe problems will arise that will astound every textbook methodology.

The world can't continue to make the current types of changes. Everything will not execute according to a textbook methodology. We must also keep in mind that people are unpredictable and do not react according to a prepared script.

A few things will remain consistent in the workplace: people who ignore situations or blame others will always be present. At some point a person possessing pertinent information will downplay the magnitude of the situation as if it is of no concern or choose to ignore an issue hoping things will simply work out. This form of attitude leads to problems getting worse, by causing the spread of blame. Someone will be "left holding the bag" along with the associated cost of repair. Prudence, wisdom, and ability to understand people are necessary resources to survival in the marketplace. People are unpredictable so knowing how to read body language, identify signs of problems in the early stages, and address and solve problems are essential tools.

When I first meet people, I am a quiet person. I prefer watching and listening to people instead of speaking. I watch how a person's body language shifts, and I will listen to the words and tones they use when talking. I have noticed that most people with experience and wisdom will not approach a subject matter as if talking about a distant relative but as an intimate friend or companion. There is no longer a beginning or an end, but a constant exchange of ideas. The expert's eyes, voice, and body will give the subject life and invite listeners to join in this intimacy intertwining the good, bad, and the ugly aspects of a topic in order to give the illusion that the intricacies of the topic are dependent upon each other. A true expert does not just speak with words; this person's entire being joins the conversation to participate in telling the story of traveling down the road of experience. They will call wisdom their dearest friend, their most treasured sister.

At this point, you may be asking how to identify someone with real wisdom. Before we move ahead, keep one thing in mind. In the workplace, a person with wisdom is unnecessary at every little level or in executing every single task. There are jobs and duties that are well-suited for people who have lots of book knowledge and can follow a process flow, standard processes, or a structure exactly, without questioning authority. These types of people need to be on the team, but we have to know where they fit the best and where they do not add value to the overall objectives of the organization.

For example, when I think about a person of wisdom, I reflect on my grandmother and the amount of wisdom she possessed being a culinary artist. Twenty years of running her own catering business and over ten years running a kitchen at Sleighton Farm Reform

School and teaching her craft gave her a unique blend of insight and wisdom for baking. On the other hand, there are those who have learned or gained a little knowledge about how to bake a cake from reading the recipe stapled to their refrigerator door. This person will approach baking a cake by methodically following a recipe. They will systematically follow the recipe, adding everything accordingly without ever questioning the steps. In short, a pseudo chef is under the impression that by following a recipe, they should end up with the same kind of moist cake as the photo on the front of the box seems to promise. Grandma always referred to this type of baker as box cake chefs.

On the contrary, Grandmother, having experience and wisdom, baked her cakes from scratch. She knew to pay attention to the little details like letting the eggs set out until they were at room temperature. She understood the difference between folding the eggs and using a blender. Moreover, she knew that by changing her methods, she could change the results. Grandmother, having the experience as well as wisdom, was able to provide guidance without even being present in the same room or city. I recall hearing her telling someone what had gone wrong with a cake they attempted to cook simply by listening to the steps they had followed and allowing the person to describe the outcome. She could even offer alternative methods to rectify what seemed like a hopeless situation. People with true experience and wisdom not only have the ability to understand the standard process, but also understand when to deviate from the norm because circumstances have changed.

Today's workforce needs all types of people to meet the current demands. You have to be transparent and honest when appointing people by fully considering their skill sets and their limitations. Do not put a person in a position requiring wisdom when all they are equipped to use is a list of instructions. Do not put a person with wisdom in a position that requires them to follow rigid protocols. Both cases will hinder these types of people from bringing true value to the organization that helps the company grow and stay competitive and profitable while providing a healthy working environment for all employees.

Who will serve well in various parts of an organization? Is it a person who is knowledgeable, an individual who is wise, or perhaps both? This will totally depend on the organization's needs, objectives, and budget. Vast numbers of people possessing vast amounts of book knowledge exist. However, only a few are capable of handling real life business needs with a particular skill set and possess genuine insight for carrying projects or assignments to the next level. Every leader and worker should ask the question whether a situation requires textbook knowledge or real wisdom and how will they bring value to the organization and its workforce. The answer to this question will lay the pathway for the leaders, the organization, and its workforce. Understand that neither age nor generation are the drivers for this type of matchmaking because it is simply about who has the wisdom or skills required.

OPINION 3

Not Everyone Understands Leadership

Contrary to popular believes I don't think everyone is a leader. I think lots of people want the glamor of being in leadership, but very few want the responsibility. Some people think good leadership can be developed by reading a few good books and attending certain training courses. I am not against good sound training and reading an insightful book, but I see them as tools to refine and build upon a strong foundation. If the foundation is weak training, reading thousands of books will not be sufficient.

I have heard it said that character is what comes out when a person is under pressure. Which raises the question to whom in an organization should people look when pressure arises? For leadership to be good, it must respond to the situation, so the correct person upon whom to depend, depends on the situation.

Subconsciously, I probably do a little bit of a personal calculation to determine just how far I am willing to follow another person. I calculate the probability of loss, the impact of that loss, and determine what I am willing to accept. In the back of my mind, I decide if I am going to whole heartily follow this particular person because the probability of loss is very low. In some cases, it's a check on my personal situation to see if something within me needs to change and whether continuing to follow this person will develop my character and experiences. Needless to say, this effort requires more time and soul searching before yielding. If the loss is too great, and no opportunity to grow exists, I make a plan B and begin thinking of a transition to something different, including moving to an entirely different situation or company that is more aligned to my career path. I don't make a proactive decision to give up on people, but I have learned from times when I should have jumped ship and failed to. I believed in a person as a leader and more than likely ignored some of the apparent signs of trouble because my mind kept telling me to stay and support the individual as a leader, show my loyalty and commitment. Consequently, I remained in situations longer than I needed or should have, and I paid the price.

Indeed, even great leaders have trouble under pressure and make considerable mistakes. However, good leaders will stand up and take even more responsibility for the outcome and recognize when they have made a mistake. They won't leave the sinking ship or organization workforce to deal with the consequences. On the contrary, a good leader would work to keep things going, hold together, and support everyone as much as possible. These types of leaders will not leave or give up hope but give their very best to help achieve the best outcome.

It may sound and looks good as part of the organization's plans to say everyone is a leader, but in reality, not everyone has the skill set or qualities necessary to be a leader. Working for a person who does not have leadership skills can lead to a very long and frustrating work week or even encourage a periodic sick day. In essence, morale gets progressively lower.

Plenty of books on leadership are available with definitions that probably, but I simply think a leader is someone who people are willing to follow. It has little to do with title, role, or position. In the workplace of today, some organizations have layers and layers of managers, but very few shepherds. People are serving in roles and positions with grand titles such as director, manager, vice-president, and president, but does anyone in the organization follow these people with confidence?

I recall an instance in a large company meeting where the CEO was being held responsible for a corporation that was on the verge of losing a lot of market shares and possibly going to be purchased by a competitor. As he stood before the crowd, I distinctly recall two things: he stood tall and confident and spoke with a calm and steady voice as he disclosed the pressures being placed upon him to deliver aggressive timelines and the growing anxiety from the board about his leadership. To the employees, filled with anxiety and mixed emotions, sitting in a standing room only hotel conference room who were mentally calculating the impact on their futures, he painted a picture of the future if he was a master painter. He painted a clear view of the options, the alternatives, and the impact on each person in the room regardless of level. As he closed his speech, his voice shifted, and he made a declaration to everyone in the room, "Now, you focus on doing your jobs while I concentrate on my job of solving this problem." In reality, the circumstances had not changed, but the room seemed to suddenly exhale and begin to breathe again and become rejuvenated. Unfortunately for him, the board of directors wanted to see things happen a little faster and appointed a new CEO.

As the organization made the transition to new leadership, it was apparent things had changed drastically, and the level of trust that previously existed had vanished. This lack of confidence affected the way people performed their duties and their level of drive and passion. People began leaving the organization by the busload. Market share started melting like ice cream in a Texas summer heat. These employees once saw themselves as being able to build a future with this corporation, yet that confidence faded as the needs of employees faded from the mind of leadership. Getting people who have one foot out the door to remain dedicated and loyal is hard, especially if the new leader has not gained their trust.

What is the difference between these two leaders? Both were viewed as leaders, but only one gained the commitment and willingness of his employees. An abrupt change in leadership can affect the morale within an organization and the productivity from employees, which can lead to people resigning and retiring or to layoffs because of the decline in production.

If we stop for a moment and honestly ponder the concept of leadership, what characteristics stand out about a real leader? History provides a massive list of people who historians consider great leaders, but what truths may be overlooked or swept under the rug?. Was it their schooling? Their level of education? Perhaps their family background, their social circle, or the amount of profit they were able to generate for the business taught them their skills. In all honesty, all of these things are nice, but I would not follow anyone simply based on any one of these qualities without some level of trust.

Additionally, I do not think all leaders look alike or hold one basic package of characteristics. In my opinion, many excellent leaders look like or identify with the problems or situations they are solving or the people who they are leading. They may not dress in the latest fashions, speak with a perfect dialect, or be the most admired amongst their peers. Truly, in most situations the people we now consider great leaders were once overlooked or considered outcasts by the peers and a majority of society. Their ability to see into the future, to plan for the unknown, and to challenge the norm made people around them uncomfortable. We want leaders to fit into a beautiful box with defined characteristics and expectations. You cannot use a cookie cutter approach to make a good leader, nor does a set list of characteristics exist by which to judge a good leader.

If you perceive yourself as a leader, turn around because someone should be following you. If no one is following you, then whom are you leading? Granted, even passing the above test does not indicate you are a great leader because history has proven even the vilest of people can generate a few followers. We honor roles and titles without argument. If a person holds a leadership position, we acknowledge that title, even if personal actions do not align with expectations for that role. In other words, if someone is a king or queen that person gets the honor because of that title. The person holding the position may not warrant this recognition; but it is not about the person, it is about the honor bestowed upon the position.

I make this point because honoring someone is different from being led by that person. Honoring can be something executed based on culture, but being led relies on trust. If I do not trust, a person's motives, I will not follow them. I see a leader as someone into whose hands I put mine with the promise they will do their best to yield the best results and take care of me. Certainly, there are times when things will not go as planned, but as long as you as a leader keep my best interest at heart as the motive, I shall surely follow. Trust is a matter of the heart, and the heart is a free will agent. If trust is absent, so is the willingness to follow. In other words, without trust, no loyalty exists, and then there will be no commitment; thus you are not leading.

Some may think that I am a little much in this area, but I would challenge them to look around at those around them. If you were honest, how many of perceived followers would stick around if the going gets rough or if a better opportunity comes along? I would also question if you are leading these people and if they are actually standing behind you or perhaps, they are just waiting for another umbrella (leader) to cover them from the showers (problems). As soon as the door of opportunity opens, the will walk out and attached themselves to another.

Every organization needs good leaders or a team of leaders with diverse characteristics, various specialties, and the ability to build trust among associates that inspires people to follow the individual leaders or the leadership team. I do not believe a business can create a sustainable organization today unless it implements a successful leadership team. Today's unique business environment makes good leadership even more important than ever.

A few generations ago, a person could start with a company and plan to retire from that same company. Today neither the employer nor the employee will entertain any expectations for building a long-term relationship. Many companies are not loyal to their employees, which reciprocates a similar feeling from the employee, thus yielding increased turnover of employees. Secondly, the world is connected by many factors, one of which is the internet. The internet increases an entrepreneur's opportunity for starting a small business that can entertain international trade opportunities. Virtual agents can work for companies from anywhere in the world remotely because of the internet. Additionally, the connectivity of a global market requires a more agile and creative work environment, thus changing the dynamics and demands of the employee skill sets. Since this workforce must be dynamic, it will need a more dynamic leadership who can create an atmosphere that drives innovation and manages diverse talent.

A substantial amount of discussion about the new workforce, with a primary focus on the Millennial generation, is available. A unique situation in the workplace today exists. However, I get a little nervous when all the media and professional advisors agree on one particular subject and go in the same direction. Historically, this type of agreement has indicated we missed something that could have a significant impact. An example is the supposed mass exodus of Baby Boomers out of the workplace into retirement. The experts apparently forgot to ask Baby Boomers about plans or consider the multiple financial crises when formulating this forecast.

Everyone thought real estate was a sure investment and that everything was going well despite all the signs. Investors kept blowing up the housing bubble so much until it expanded its capacity and burst taking with it the financial future and security of many innocent bystanders. After the real estate market crashed, everyone claimed they saw it coming. If all these people who claimed they saw this crash coming and knew something was going to happen had spoken up, I wonder if we could have tolerated the noise. In reality the few soft voices warning about the pitfalls of the practices that led to the crash were silenced by all the other voices cheering to keep the party going, which we did at a high cost.

What will be the bubble that bursts tomorrow? What is sitting silent behind the noise of the new Millennial workforce waiting to explode and bring about another destructive implosion of the marketplace? The Millennial generation is part of the current workforce and having an impact on how work is being done, but they are not the full story.

Effective leaders have to be able to see what others are unable to see and close out the noise to hear the distinct quiet voice of wisdom. They must be able to discern how all the parts of the business fit together, interact, and affect the overall operations of an organization. The workforce is crucial, and the Millennial generation is part of this labor force, but what are the hidden things not easily seen or understood by the larger population? It will be the ability to discern and have the prudence to plan affectively that will detect the great leaders of today and tomorrow.

Sphere of Influence

There is a misconception that effective leadership in one area easily transfers to something else. A leader should understand their sphere of influence and know that influence in one area may not transfer to another. Great leaders seem to be connected in some fashion to their field of influence. Perhaps they are assimilated to those they lead or those who they lead assimilate to them. Whatever the process, the result is an intimate connection or marriage.

A marriage in which loyalty and trust between the parties exist. The strong voice speaks on behalf of those who are unable to speak, or their voices are unheard. The leader steps forward with passion, determination, and unselfishness driving a vision larger than themselves. Perhaps misunderstood, unconventional, and unordinary but yet driven by their passion and connection to the people for whom they are advocating or who they are representing.

In some cases, a leader may not be leading a group of people, but a vision, and the people are merely impacted as a consequence. People following the vision inadvertently follow the leader. However, the marriage is not between the leader and the people but the leader and the vision, which probably explains why some leaders seem so disconnected from people. Perhaps it is because the people are merely a product of the marriage between leader and vision.

Steve Jobs, cofounder of Apple, was viewed as a difficult person and insensitive to those around him. However, no one can disagree that his drive and vision produced changes to the way technology has been integrated into daily life and changed other industries such as music. His vision developed a platform for individuals to create and share their ideas through the Apple store. Millions of people around the world have benefited and prospered from the marriage between this leader and his vision.

George Westinghouse, on the other hand, believed it was his calling to open up companies to provide opportunities and jobs for his employees. Leadership based on a marriage between himself and his employees consequently drove a vision to create multiple businesses. In this case, the vision was a product of the marriage between a leader and the people.[7] Whether leading people, vision, or cause, it is imperative for a leader to understand limits, influence, and power. Wrong assumptions can lead to disappointments, discouragement, rage, or failure.

Dr. Martin Luther King Jr. led the Civil Rights cause, but the people benefited. If his heart had been set on leading a group of people, he might have been highly disappointed. In reality, he didn't have much support during the early years of the movement especially from those of his community. In fact, some of the followers of Dr. King did not look like him and were not direct victims of the oppression felt by members of the black community. In his famous, "I Have a Dream" speech, Dr. King revealed to whom he is married – the cause – equality for all humankind. The marriage to the cause drove him to endure the hardships he encountered as a leader and consequently changed the nation. Any illusion of marriage to the people would have probably ended up in a divorce and no change for our country or the people.

How does any leader know whether they are connected to vision, people, or cause? Perhaps, examine what keeps them moving past obstacles. It may sound great to say the people, but in most cases, this is not the truth. They are merely the benefactors of a marriage.

Society may cast a leader committed to a cause or vision as selfish and try to persuade that leader to change their alliance to the people who are being led, which might seem more acceptable. A Leader who is married to the people posses a great gift. Leaders who are married to people seem to possess a special gift to ignore those people's shortcomings, dismiss disloyal behavior, and find good.

Perhaps the reason there are so many issues in the workplace is because leaders are being forced to marry or connected to the workforce when it is the vision or cause to which their loyalty stands. If my natural gift is visionary, then I am naturally going to be passionate about the vision, and my thoughts, decision, and actions will most likely align with that vision. Consequently, this may come across as insensitive and problematic to the people I am leading because they have marriage expectations that will not be fulfilled. Like any marriage, there is a level of expectation established from the beginning, and when these expectations are not met, problems develop in the relationship for all parties. However, if I understand it is the vision to which I am married I will have different expectations of the people and be wise about the expectations they set for me as a leader. Perhaps I bring in another person who is more gifted at connecting with people and can fill in that gap while I focus on the vision.

If a leader deeply connects with one of the three: vision, people, or a cause, that leader should not ignore the other areas. Be aware of actions, decisions, and directions that are driven more by one area than the others and make an attempt to balance out these other areas by understanding the needs and finding other leaders to fill the gaps.

Everyone wants to be in a leadership position, but very few can fill the role with great success. I believe situations call forth great leaders. Ulysses S. Grant, a commanding General in the Union Army and the 18th President of United States, stated something along these lines regarding three types of leaders in battle. One type rushes to the front of the battle line because he wants spotlight, only to be instantly killed; the second type is scared and reluctant to go to front line and gets instantly killed because of fear; and the third type is reluctant but goes to the front line leading simply due to circumstances and has success because he is forced to lead. Grant saw himself as the third type.[8] Many great leaders probably never imagined themselves on the front line leading vision, people, or cause, but circumstances or situations called, and they answered.

---

[7] Jansen Media Studio; Director: Mark Bussler. 2009. *Westinghouse: The Life & Times of an American Icon* . Amazon.
[8] Grant, Ulysses S. 1885.. *Personal Memories of U.S. Grant*. Charles L Webster & Co (New York). eBook published by Project Gutenberg.

OPINION 4

Management Skills Are Not Gained Through Promotion

Steve sat tucked into a small comfortable corner, eyes diligently piercing through a set of thin black wired framed lenses, which were slowly making their way to the edge of his nose. In one succinct motion, he gingerly pushed the glasses back to the crest of his nose and turned the page of the large bound report resting on his desk between a sea of the previous versions of the same report. Oblivious to the constant flow of traffic dropping off and picking up papers and the crowd of black suits assembling around, his eyes remained glued to the numbers and the steady rhythm as he punched numbers into the desk calculator. The black suits had emerged from a large scenic office aligning the walls and swarmed to Steve's desk like bees to honey. They were awaiting the current month's sales outcomes. The expectations for Steve's role were simple: gather data, calculate, prepare reports, distribute, and know the information. At the end of the day, he went home and came back the next day to do it all again. Two things remained constant in his organization: change and his role. That is until the company was acquired by a competitor and new leadership emerged.

Interrupting his routine his desk phone suddenly rang. A human resources representative was on the other end. The HR representative told Steve that he had been running his department so well that leadership has decided it was time for him to be promoted. The sales reports had impressed the vice president in charge of sales. Steve was being made responsible for the northeast region of company sales. As the HR representative continued to speak, Steve's mind began to reflect back a few days prior when one of the black suits stopped by his desk and spoke. He had asked Steve a few questions about the report and its content then turned and walked away. As Steve gently returned the phone to the receiver, a light thought danced across his mind. "Department! What department? It's just me and the number crunching part-time guy."

Two weeks later while standing behind a long curtain, Steve began to slowly scan the room of attendees. Faces seemed vaguely familiar, but he found himself unable to precisely place names to the faces. Steve recognized a woman sitting in the front row wearing a striped blue suit and white blouse. No longer were there stacks of papers or tan walls of a cubicle obstructing his view, however, these were the faces of the suits who had once stood like bees waiting for the infamous sales report. Now their eyes were bright, steady, and attentive as the speaker began to shift the focus of his presentation. Still focusing his attention on the audience Steve barely noticed the speaker actions until his words began to penetrate his thoughts. "Now, ladies and gentlemen, please help me welcome our newest Manager of the Northeast Sales Region, ..."

In reality, this scenario probably does not play out exactly like this in real life. However, many times individuals are thrust into new roles with high expectations placed on them with little to no experience with managing and relating to people. Some say that experience comes from having the opportunity to do. I agree, but just because a person has had some success in one area does not mean that they are prepared to oversee the work of others and dictate job responsibilities I believe that top managers have special qualities that make them stand out from someone who merely carries the title of manager. A good leader should know how to manage people well and understand how to push a person to excel. A real leader challenges an employee to go beyond their perceived limits and supports and encourages that employee to do their very best.

While working in the finance division of a company, I had a manager who felt it was his responsibility to coach himself out of a job. Chris was a seasoned corporate accountant who spoke as if everything he said was written as law. Once Chris had articulated an idea if no one with authority or evidence could change his mind, Chris's idea was considered a forgone conclusion, and no further discussion was conducted. At that point, if the topic came up again, it was merely an update. I could gauge Chris's opinion of my work by the amount of time he felt required to look over my shoulder. If I saw Chris a lot, that was not good. If I did not see him very often, I considered that as a reward and a sign that I was doing a good job. He did not say much and barely gave me any direct positive feedback, but if I missed the mark, I heard about it. Despite these experiences, I still think of Chris as one of the best managers for whom I ever had the pleasure of knowing. Working with him challenged me to open my eyes and see people and face uncomfortable situations.

One day during our regularly scheduled check-in, I happened to ask Chris how he grew up. It wasn't on our agenda, and I didn't plan on asking the question before going into the room, but once in his office, it popped into my mind. Shifting slightly in his seat across the desk he started to share a little about how he grew up in New York City. This routine became part of our regular agenda. I would ask a little about his background, and he would share, then we moved on to the business at hand. This exchange helped me understand more about him and how he viewed certain things, and I gained a better understanding of how to work with him. At times the messages were not always delivered in nice pretty packages, but since I knew more about him I understood the heart behind his words, and I learned what to ignore. Nevertheless, I always knew his level of trust in my abilities. I realize that this type of management style may not work for everyone, and I am not suggesting it should. In fact, an opportunity did I arise where I was able to give Chris some feedback on how he communicated with others. Contrary to what others would have expected, he received the feedback and began making a few changes on how he dealt with the people he managed. It wasn't that he wasn't willing to make changes; people just assumed he wouldn't and never bothered giving him feedback. Our business relationship grew stronger, and he still did not hesitate to let me know when I missed the mark.

I can recall an instance when Chris called me into his office to address a communication problem I was having with a few of my team leaders. In a nutshell, these team leaders and I didn't particularly care for one another, and the irritation and disrespect were growing throughout the team and impacting our ability to work together and behave professionally. Chris openly voiced his opinion challenging my handling of a situation with one particular member of the team. Even though he listened to my side of the story, he proceeded to chide me about how it was imperative I fix the problem. By no means was the exchange in his office comfortable. In fact, it felt as if the office got smaller and smaller by the minute. I was not comfortable with confrontation, and Chris knew it. He even offered at one point to step in and intervene if I thought it would be helpful. I gave him my assurance I would not delay and marched out of his office to the other person's office to face the problem right away. Chris knew if I didn't address the problem it would only get worse. He taught me a treasured lesson that day about how to handle office politics and survive even during the most uncomfortable challenges. I learned not to dance around a problem or allow it to last longer than necessary. In retrospect, he was grooming me to be a leader by teaching me how to deal with confrontations effectively. I learned a hard lesson from experience, not from reading a book.

In my opinion, an excellent manager understands how to keep his ship running despite rough seas. An astute manager knows the exact words that push an employee to do a little more, work a little harder, give just a bit more effort. Yet, within the same moment, an excellent manager will also know when to look out for an employee's best interest and show their contributions are valued. Most people can be encouraged to give their best efforts during tough circumstances because they want to deliver their best for a leader they respect.

I don't want to give the impression that good managers perform flawlessly every day, excellent at managing people with little to no mistakes, and perform perfectly in every aspect of being a leader. Nothing could be further from the truth. Many of the people who I consider as having been good at managing people made mistakes often. However, I was consistently impressed by how they fixed mistakes or admitted shortcomings to their staff and kept moving forward. They lived by the philosophy that life goes on, and a problem or mistake doesn't stop progress: learn from mistakes and keep moving. If the business begins to have problems you may need another plan but don't lose sight of the big picture for the sake of focusing on small stuff.

Some people are terrible at handling staff in high-pressure situations, especially during a crisis. As a result, they get nervous and search for something they can control, end up focusing time and energy on the smallest problem and creating a big deal out of nothing. Because they have no idea how to handle the major issue, or would rather try to ignore its existence, they obsess about a small one. Perhaps they hope if a major issue is ignored long enough, it will work itself out or a situation will present itself to allow the problem to be passed along to someone else. I do not enjoy working for a manager who takes this tact.

People are both excellent and problematic at all levels of an organization and in all types of organizations. Someone will always be there who can pull the best and worst out of coworkers or employees. Everyone must learn, regardless of their level in the hierarchy of the organization, how to control themselves and the impact others have on their actions and thoughts. Over the years I hope to perfect the gift of ignoring things that frustrate me. There are some things people do I need to just learn to ignore. Imagine how the workplace would be if we developed the gift of ignoring every single thing that irked me. A co-worker may walk up to another and say," Hey, did you see what she just did." The response would be, "Nope, I am perfecting my gift of ignore."

A co-worker, " Don't you care."

The response, "Nope."

If managers and leaders at all levels could perfect this gift, they would probably have more time at the end of the day. The large things aren't what consume time and energy at the office but the little petty disputes and behaviors that make their way into the office culture.

I have often heard it said that people become better managers with experience. To some extent, I agree. However, a few things need to inform upon that idea. Managers are not dealing with inanimate objects; they are dealing with real people. People have feelings, emotions, and needs, and one of those needs is the need to feel valued. People react better, and in most cases produce at a higher level, when they are treated with honor and respect. People will not change bad habits or undesirable behaviors if they continue to be promoted to higher levels in the organization despite continuing to display bad habits. This style of promotion sends the wrong message to the rest of the organization. A person who starts as a bad manager and never receives proper training will develop into a weak leader as they move up in the ranks. Poor management skills can stay hidden for a period, but I guarantee, as these weak managers rise to the top of the organization, such weak management will become costly for the company, particularly due to improper exchanges with staff, coworkers, or customers.[1]

People with bad management skills can improve skills over time and with training, but they have to have the willingness in their heart to change. Mistakes will happen as people learn, and most people forgive managers who are willing to improve and receive proper training.

Training programs are a great resource to build strong foundations of leadership skills. When managers understand foundational skills that they nurture over time to become part of their routine and behavior, they become strong managers and a valuable commodity for an organization. Old habits take time to correct even when people are willing to make changes, so expectations regarding skill development must be reasonable. A person shouldn't expect to attend training one week and suddenly become the greatest manager of all time. Once a high-pressure situation arises, natural behaviors will rise to the surface, so it takes time to undo bad habits and create new better habits and behaviors.

Very few good employees will remain at an organization and continue to be productive if they are consistently mistreated. Competitors will always be willing to hire employees with training and skills from a competing business. The competitor gets a willing and trained employee who can come into a new environment and begin contributing to the bottom line almost immediately. It's a win for both the competitor and the employee, and a loss for the company that the employee left.

Additionally, a manager's inability to interact well with coworkers and staff may also bleed through to interactions with customers. Some of the airlines I am forced to fly due to travel schedule and business location demonstrate this fact because I can see by the interaction between staff that the morale in the company is low. Any chance I get at taking another airline, even if it sometimes means an extra layover or an additional cost, I take because my comfort when traveling is more important. Customers enjoy being treated well, and an organization's employees are the primary representatives of the company. If employees are not happy, it will pour over onto customers. Generations have had problems with receiving excellent customer service, but it was the Millennial generation that took hold of the social media tools and made a small voice vast and effective.[3] As a result, organizations of all sizes have begun to implement various methods and tools to ensure the customer experience is positive and that the voice of the customer is heard and responded to.

Similarly, a friend shared how she was working with a hospital to develop new training for the hospital staff on interacting with patients. Primarily, she was training hospital staff how to display a caring and more engaged attitude toward patients. Apparently our society has gotten to the point where a training course is necessary to teach individuals the things we used to learn growing up, that is to treat others with honor and respect.

In reality, everyone wants to be treated with respect, and it has nothing to do with age, social status, or education. When people are honored and respected they respond differently than when they are not treated with honor and respect. Organizations that value their employees at all levels, and their customers, benefit by employing people who practice good human interaction skills and integrating those people into the fabric of the organization.

Organizations also benefit by helping leaders use skills to managing people beyond just motivating them in performance. Strong leaders understand how to pull the best out of their staff. They identify and nurture the strengths of others and hold meaningful conversations. They invest in developing skills in others and building future leaders, which is more than just overseeing work. It is making a sacrifice to think more about another person than oneself and putting that person before your needs at times. Being less focus on just simply driving results, goals, metrics, deliverables, key performance metrics, or financial results and more concern for developing better people, better employees, and delivering a better service to customers. I had the pleasure of working for one leader who simply thought it was her duty to take care of the people she managed, and the business results would follow. Consequently, developing a staff saturated with leaders and an organization excited about opportunities contributed to a bigger vision; she spent less time correcting and more time innovating, and that was a great workplace.

In the workplace today employees expect feedback and coaching to help them develop in their careers.[1] However, if their leader has historically been more focused on results than people, this leader may not understand how to develop members of their team. It is sometimes assumed that a member of leadership inherently commands these skills. But that is not the case. Traditionally people have been trained how to produce, achieve goals, and grow a business. People have not been trained how to develop the skills of others and operate with care and honor while caring out all the other demands of business.

In most cases, if a person in leadership displays leadership skills it's considered a natural gift, perhaps part of their personality or natural skill set. Many in today's business world feel leadership qualities are absent from the younger generation.[1] However, I don't believe this characteristic has been any more prevalent in other generations. In fact, it's probably been about the same or worse. From our very beginning as a child, our common human instinct is self-survival, but as we grow older, we hopefully learn to care for others.

Self-absorption is not a common trait among leaders who understand how to manage teams and push members to achieve great results both personally and professionally. Leaders who know how to motivate teams to achieve and still encourage the team members to feel supported, loved, and honored possess qualities built on the foundation of serving others. Exceptional leadership is based upon the foundation of being a good servant, caring for others, and understanding that with greater power, the higher you go in an organization, comes greater responsibility and a higher expectation to serve.

Skills are not obtained by a simple promotion from one level of management to another. A person does not move from staff to manager to director and suddenly become endowed with super abilities and an understanding of how to manage people. Some leadership skills come naturally, and some can be taught, but the foundation of the heart is not established on serving others it is bound to be ineffective; at least in relation to interacting with people.

In summary, great leadership and management skills are not a factor of age or title. There are people of all ages and generations who are poor leaders and managers. On the flip side of that coin, there are people of all ages and generations who are great leaders and managers. Some skills must be learned through experience, and experience can only be gained over time. People are not plug-n-play, which means dealing with them will change from one incident to another, from one organization to another, and from one individual to another. However, those with a heart to serve others tend to figure out more quickly than their counterparts. Their willingness to serve and care for others seems to translate into the wisdom needed to address the challenges faced in a leadership role.

---

[1] Seppanen, S.S., and W. Gualtieri. National Chamber Foundation. 2012. *The Millennial Generation Research Review*.
[3] Deloitte 2016 Millennial Survey. *Winning over the next Generation of Leaders*.

OPINION 5

Commitment Has Changed Its Look

If the parameters that defined "commitment" for the workplace in the past have changed, is that so bad? Perhaps the measure of commitment depends on surrounding circumstances, and maybe what made the characteristics of commitment important to an organization in the past is no longer significant.

If I am taking a taxi in New York City the commitment level between the cab driver and me is probably really low. Sure I have expectations they will drive me to my destination safely and operate the taxi in the proper mind and condition to deliver on those expectations. As a result, I commit to paying a fee for the service. If the driver falls short of this, the commitment we had to one another is not life threatening. Perhaps, costly, irritating, and inconvenient, but in New York City, I can find other alternative travel choices.

In business organizations today, the level of commitment in the workplace has changed from previous generations. In the past, when a person joined a company, it was the same as being involved in a family, a working family with whom an individual planned to be associated for a long time. Annually, the leader of the organization would share a long-range plan, which included the role each employee was expected to play in these plans of the organization. Mostly, unspoken was the understanding that the company would take care of its employees if the employees returned this commitment. Sounds like something from a movie, but for the most part, this is what people believed. Go to school. Get hired by a good company; stay there until you retire.

Have things changed in the workplace to such a degree that we no longer see the same level of commitment as we experienced in the past? Younger generations are perceived as a flight risk and less likely to remain with an employer long term.[1] Perhaps the findings in the studies are correct, or maybe it's a consequence of a work culture or workplace that is changing. The business world is more global and more connected than in previous generations. Organizations are outsourcing more entry-level jobs and transactional based positions that used to be filled by less experienced staff who would have been starting their commitment to the organization. Also, organizations are no longer limited to candidates in their local markets or regions to fill available roles or positions but can now extend their reach globally, which means they don't have to spend the years grooming management candidates.[4]

Many organizations no longer function with a workforce viewed as or treated like family planted in one general location building relationships over the years. Instead, workforces are spread continents apart, through multiple time zones and have various cultural differences. Workforces may consist of a mixture of traditional employees, hired staff who work for multiple organizations, and consultants who are hired to support specific projects on a short-term basis.

Although how business organizations view their workforces may be different than in the past, this does not necessarily indicate that how they view their workforces in today's work environment is wrong. Alteration of the expectations of how work gets done today as compared to past generations is necessary and clearly defining the roles and requirements of all parties so that each understands the degree of commitment required of them is essential. This way both employers and employees understand the consequences and risk levels if promises are not kept.

The workplace today has changed and continues to change. In the business sector, competition is broader and changing constantly, customer expectation is consistently evolving, and economics of the world are changing and influencing the market globally. Today, everything from global monetary policy, wars, and emerging companies affect business forecasts. In today's business world if an employer does not keep up with the current marketing trends, they could end up closing their doors. The new millennium is proving to be challenging than what our ancestors faced fifty years ago. For some employees, this development could be an incredibly invigorating period of opportunity in the workplace: a lowered level of commitment, no certain obligations, stay with an employer as long the job is enjoyable, and then move on. However, for those who have been in the workforce longer, this may cause anxiety, fear, and questions about loyalty. How much blood, sweat, and tears do you give to a company that may sell the division or outsource the department? A flexible workforce is desirable in many ways, but if a majority of employees have never held a job longer than one or two years, how do these employees understand how to develop and cultivate long-term vision?

I am not saying this change in commitment is entirely bad, especially given the business world of today. I do believe it changes the landscape of how we do business, how the employer to employee relationship plays out, and how we should approach business planning and strategy. Market experts guess or predict how this trend will influence business models in the future, and what under this current model trend might look like best methods and practices as well as desirable outcomes. New problems can't be fixed by studying them through old lenses or prescribing archaic solutions. Problems today may look different than the ones from previous generations, but when we begin to pull back the layers, the same core items, granted repackaged with new labels, appear.

Organizations and their employees will need to adapt to these changes by viewing them through new lenses. Some employers loved the relationship they had with employees. Unfortunately, they can no longer afford this level of commitment to all roles or positions in the organization, and they must choose which jobs are long term and which can sustain more turnover. These temporary roles or transactional roles can be filled by consultants, freelancers, or temporary or short-term employees. The level of commitment may sway, and the details of the relationship and cost of impact must be clearly documented and understood by all parties. Employees must understand where they stand with their employers. It's not beneficial for either party to believe that a long-term commitment has been made, when in reality, it has not. Unfortunately, more victims of this misunderstanding are starting to occupy our streets holding signs with a variety of phrases but the same message – victim of a bad corporate divorce. Although discussions about longevity in the workplace may be uncomfortable for both the employer and the employee, it's better to be transparent and let everyone know where they actually stand in the employer-employee relationship.

The answers do not solely rest on the shoulders of any one party or generation; everyone is learning how to function and operate in a world that is constantly changing. Change requires new skills, and since many don't understand this future business model, it is probably safe to say new skills are going to be needed by everyone. All generations are going to have to learn to work together and support one another. Those with experience will need to help those who lack adequate skills and experience, which crosses all generations.[4]

The business world does not need another source of separation between two groups of people. I can't predict how things will look in the coming years, but I do believe the sustaining leaders will understand the value of the workforce they manage or lead, clearly communicate the level of commitment, and successfully nurture a strong workforce. How commitment is defined and then how expectations grow around that definition will also probably change. Perhaps employers will commit to taking care of people regardless of whether they are career employees, temporary or short-term employees or consultants. Perhaps employees will commit to doing an excellent job and delivering their very best regardless of whether the employment situation in a long-term career job, temporary or short-term, or a contracted client. Commitment has changed its style to align with the fabric of today's workforce, and it's not a bad thing just different.

---

[1] Seppanen, S.S., and W. Gualtieri. National Chamber Foundation. 2012. *The Millennial Generation Research Review*.
[4] World Economic Forum Report. 2016. *Future of Jobs*.

OPINION 6

Hidden Issues Cause Damage

The word "accountable" is defined as "required to explain actions or decisions to someone or required to be responsible for something." In other words, a level of responsibility to another person is an integral piece of the idea behind the meaning of this word. Essentially, another person or persons will be involved or impacted by the actions of another. Thus, being accountable means thinking of others. Leaders of organizations are assumed to be responsible individuals; consequently, these leaders receive the trust from the board of directors, shareholders, employees, and customers that they will carry out their duties with integrity and to the benefit of others. Unfortunately, in recent events, the actions of leaders of organizations have painted a different picture on the canvas of the public mind.

Consider a situation when the leader of a company raises the price for medication overnight for profit regardless of public scrutiny. Such as the boy genius Martin Shkreli, who price gouged a drug for AIDS and cancer patients. The price went from $13.50 to $750 overnight. The CEO of Turing Pharmaceuticals defended a 5,000 percent increase for a life-saving pill. In the end, he ended up becoming the "most hated man in America" for fifteen minutes. Some CEOs like Shkreli enjoy providing the impression that they are not accountable for their actions. They like to fall back on the adage: "Profit justifies the means."

Martin Shkreli's decision may be attributed to his age—he was 32 years old when these events happened—which leads inevitably to the question of whether the Millennial generation is insensitive and selfish.[1] Millennials are generally acknowledged to be one of the most caring of all generations due to their infectious drive to establish social economic organizations and address the needs of the poor rather than solely focusing on economic gain.[3]

Perhaps, social conscious and empathy are different between generations, or is the packaging in which the passions are delivered today just different? Once unwrapped, are Millennial efforts to establish nonprofits and nongovernment organizations the same as for other generations, particularly the Baby Boomer generation? Each generation can name a group saturated with a passion for change and driven to impact the lives of those less fortunate. One generation wears the uniform of tie-dye and platform shoes, while another chooses khakis and canvas shoes or loafers. Despite the style of one generation compared to another, at the core, the passions, and desires to help others remain the same. Ultimately, no matter the structure of the organization or the clothing of the leader, understanding the values of a given organization and holding its decision makers accountable for their actions is vital.

As a child, my mother taught me to be responsible for my actions. A situation arose where I had to make a hard decision that caused my mother to pull me aside to have one of those one-on-one sessions. There was a family trip planned a weekend I desired to remain home and hang out with a few of my friends. My parents were divorced, which meant I spent weekends away from my schoolmates and the weekend activities that were normally the topic of lunch on Monday. As I hit my teen years the desire to bond with schoolmates grew more than my desire to hang around family. This is the situation that prompted my request to forgo the family weekend trip.

My mothers' words were: "Now, think carefully about what you are going to do and decide if you can live with the consequences of your decision regardless of how it turns out." I remember stopping to think carefully through every possible scenario and became more at peace that I could deal with the outcome. Part of the process included informing my father about my decision and being able to sustain his response. Sunday night came, and I recall my mother watching to see how I was going to handle the effects of my Friday decision. My brother returned excited about the weekend and elated to show me all of the cool gifts he had received and tell me about the good time he had on the trip. As my brother danced away with his new toys, my mother asked if I was all right. I told her that, yes, I was all right, but I had to do a mental check to confirm and audit myself for envy and jealousy. After a few minutes, I could even more confidently answer that I was really fine. I had survived all the consequences of my decision.

Growing up in the business world I made an incorrect assumption that others were taught the same painful lesson of being responsible for their actions by their mothers. I realized not everyone had an opportunity to be influenced by my dear mother, but surely, their own mothers taught them the simple lessons of consequences. Instead, it appears that we have come to a time when people take action and have no regrets for the consequences of their decisions. It is as if everyone has suddenly become tightrope walkers from the circus ready to take the chance of a lifetime and risk it all. People are not taking the time to calculate the impact their decisions have on themselves, their family, or others. It seems that many will say, "Let's take a chance to see what will happen, if it works - good, if not – oh well." It would seem they would hear the small voice of

Values say, "Hey buddy don't do that because not only will you harm yourself, but others will be impacted."

However, values, at least real values, are not something a person can pick up at the department store or online. From birth, values are sown into the fabric of each individual's character. Character is the power engine that drives actions, and actions are the launch pad for an understanding of consequence and accountability. To sum it up: it all connects.

In the business world, corporate values can be plastered in every place from the restroom to a website, but if those values aren't part of an employee's DNA when they are first hired, then they will more than likely not adhere to the company's core values consistently. At times, a new hire will put on their best behavior or play the role trying to impress a senior officer. Pressure invariably brings a person's guard down and exposes real values, at which time the lack of corporate values will show. Imagine being under a very tight deadline to complete a high-profile project that could lead to a promotion. A problem arises that could delay delivery, but if left unattended such problem would not be noticed in the short-term. Consequently, a decision is made to pretend the situation does not exist but merely brush it under the rug or pretend it does not exist. Work diligently to refocus the attention of others and pretend the problem or situation does not exist.

Growing up on the east coast I experienced long winters, so as kids, our imaginations got creative on how to keep entertained inside the house. One day my brothers and I were playing around near the foyer steps of our grandmother's house despite constantly having been told not to do so. Lining the wall, down the staircase leading to the front door were tall glass vases with very delicate mouths on the top. Today, I don't recall which one of us actually hit the vase, but during an action drive, a vase was hit causing it to fall over and land on the wooden floor breaking off a piece of the opening. Quickly we ran over to examine the damage, making sure we kept excitement down so we would not draw any attention. Luckily, it was a clean break with no shattering. So, we very gently lifted up the broken peace, gingerly returned it back to the top of the vase and returned the vase to its original position on the stairs. Perfect!

A few days later our uncle came rushing through the front door and accidentally hit the exact same vase and off went the top. He began to profusely apologize to our grandmother as he tried to replace the head. Over and over again he just kept saying, "I don't know how it happened. I just barely touched it." This exchange carried on for about ten minutes with no help from a few bystanders reluctant to volunteer any information. In fact, I may have been out of college before I told my mother the real story. At the time our uncle seemed a much better candidate to take the fall and handle the consequences than either of us. As children we had not mastered the revelation of good character, telling the truth, and being responsible for our actions. We were most concerned with protecting ourselves and avoiding the price of paying for our actions. It seemed fine to allow our uncle to take the fall since chances were the repercussions on him would not be as severe.

Fortunately, for most people, these are childhood behaviors that are weaned away and replaced by more responsible natures and characters. Character is shaped and molded by values and revelations about honesty and empathy. Although my glass vase experience was not detrimental, if the habit of cheating and covering up becomes habitual, the consequences could be far worse when the truth is revealed.

In the San Francisco area, it was time to replace the famous Bay Bridge (a bridge used to connect San Francisco to East Bay cities such as Oakland and Berkeley). A contractor working on the project decided to cut costs and use less expensive materials. The plan appeared to succeed until problems began on the newly opened multi-billion-dollar bridge. As things were investigated, it was revealed materials used did not meet industry specifications.[7] Needless to say, the problem was no longer hidden, and the consequences of this action could have been detrimental especially in an earthquake environment.

Unfortunately, the values behind such behavior don't raise a question until they create a costly problem, hit the press, or cause a major catastrophe. People don't wake up one morning, get dressed, and forget to slip on their values just before heading out the door. Values are not garments one puts on, a pill swallowed, a super power energy drink, nor a slogan on a wall. Values are embedded into our characters from childhood and under geared every decision, choice, and action we make. Our beliefs, environment, and culture develop the nature of these values – the good, bad, and ugly. In essence, they are the seeds that produce the fruit of our values. If the seed is bad, the fruit will be bad. If the seed is good, the fruit will be good. If a person grows up believing stealing, killing, or destroying is wrong; their values will bear witness in their actions. If you grow up thinking the only way to rise to the top is to steal and cheat, your values and actions will be a witness.

Today's workforce is saturated with discussions on values and the need for organizational values to align with individual values. This alignment seems to drive levels of commitment, job satisfaction, and the measure of satisfaction with an employer. If an employer's values don't align with an individual employee's values, that employee can leave that workplace and search for another.[3] This philosophy implies that like people, organizations have their own sets of values.

Organizations are not raised by parents nor do they raise others but merely gather and utilize talents and skills to help meet the company objectives. People are gathered through the hiring process, which is a process that assumes an employee is qualified to help achieve the goals of the organization and will align with the core values established for the body. Organizations list core values and the people of the organization integrate the values. The process of hiring is simply a search for people who have the organization core values in their own personal set of values. Anyone can fake certain behaviors for a period of time, but under pressure, true nature and the real values will be revealed. Pressure and time have a way of unveiling the truth. How an organization will function is a summation of its leaders, and employees are a summation of their leaders. The truth is a summation of all.

In reality, people tend to buckle under pressure if they are not adequately prepared. Their real personality comes forth, and more than likely not in a way that represents the company's values, this, in turn, could damage the company's reputation. As you hear about various corporate scandals coming to the surface, do you ever wonder if anything is ever a surprise? Do you think any of the people involved in corporate scandals simply woke up one morning and suddenly decide to embezzle money. The seeds of dishonest, unethical behavior obviously already existed before the actual crime was committed. Signs of an employee's odious values more than likely showed up much earlier but were ignored because the person showed great promise and potential benefit for the company. As a result, the rest of the workforce deemed him untouchable, closed their eyes, and went on about their daily routine.

Truth can be a silent voice and a violent destroyer. The dishonesty is like the silent cancer of a business: an organization may never know dishonesty is growing inside of it until it is too late to treat it without perhaps killing the entire body. Think about all those big companies with a large success like Lehman Brothers, which suddenly disappeared. What was their unforeseen truth? The future is scary, and no one accurately knows how the future will look. Therefore, fix what I can see, prepare for what I know, and pretend I don't see the truth.

Many things will change over the years, but one thing will not change: the truth will rise to the surface at some point in time, yet be mindful that it may do so quietly. People seem to be promoted today by what they can make happen quickly to impact the present. Unfortunately, level of experience and values only seem to matter if they contribute to resolving the problems currently visible.

The topic of values today has seemed to become more confusing than previous generations. Our US culture suggests values can shift. We have questions about what is right and wrong, and people challenge other people who have values contrary to their own or disagree with their perspectives. Often shifts in culture accepted values are attributed to the change in times, but I don't believe time alters core values. Sure, individuals mature and gain a greater understanding of self and the world, but core values should never drastically change as often as one changes their shoes. In my opinion, people who easily or readily shift what they profess to be their core values are my unreliable friends. It's not always necessary to remove them or disengage from them, but you had better be honest with yourself about their loyalty and reliability and manage expectations for those traits. If our values conflict, we will probably have different perspectives on many issues but this does not mean we cannot work together.

The question is not whether coworkers agree or disagree but does that disagreement impede the ability to accomplish a common goal?

If the answer is yes, those two people won't be able to achieve a common goal then they should probably go separate ways. On the other hand, if they can find a way to stay focused on a common cause and move forward, reaching a shared goal should be as easy as it would be for two people with everything in common. Even with a very diverse workplace today, coworkers should be able to find common ground in which they can operate comfortably. Acknowledge the fact that everyone at work does not have to feel like a 'Best Friend,' nor do we necessarily need to hang out. Just ensure we are clear on our core values and the common goal.

Understanding and respecting each other's core values comes from spending quality time together, holding real conversations, and getting to know one another. In a social media age, a false sense of friendship and bonding has been developed through online "friendships." Just because I read your messages on Twitter, "like" you on Facebook, or look at your photos on Instagram does not necessarily mean we have developed a strong or real bond. It means we have connected on social media. Our conversations are virtual and limited to a few characters. In reality, we may very well have quite different values. This false sense of bonding flows from our personal lives onto the workplace. We believe we know and understand one another by a few simple exchanges, but in reality, our true natures remain hidden and unknown.

This can raise problems in our personal lives with false expectations, but in the workplace, it creates a different dynamic of challenges. In the hidden corners of organizations rest other issues growing quietly and spreading deep roots. As a result of more virtual or remote exchanges, the ability to interact and handle conflict or confrontation face to face has begun to fade. Many problems in the workplace could be resolved quickly if people simply stopped texting, instant messaging, and emailing, got up from their seat or picked up a phone and had a conversation. As adults, talk out the situation and address the problem immediately instead of allowing bad feelings to fester or circumstances to grow worse over time.

Ignored problems do not disappear; they become worse over time or get buried beneath the endless busy corporate activities. Many organizations face an inability to deal with truth or the ability to conduct an investigation into the cause of problems. Dealing with some problems can be uncomfortable, but it is necessary. Often passing a problem down to someone else is an easier method of dealing with it than solving it. Most people do not like confrontations or dealing with uncomfortable situations, and consequently, sometimes difficult questions don't get asked. If questions are not raised, no one is held accountable for addressing and resolving the problem. And, just because something is not making lots of noise or seems to be dormant does not mean it is not a problem. In reality, a big problem could be content being silent while continuing its cancerous growth.

But, most problems in the workplace are not well hidden. In truth, a simple walk around the workplace may reveal a few things. Speak with staff at all levels of the organization and various functions. For example, talking to the local door person, security personnel, a cleaning person, or the receptionist would probably be a good place to start. It's amazing the information that employees, who other employees consider invisible, have and the amount of organizational angst they can hear and see. These employees are great sources for opinions on organizational leadership.

Watch how people interact with others at all levels, watch how they approach and solve problems, watch how they share the credit or encourage others, and watch how they respond to pressure. I was never a big talker during meetings. In fact, I think it should be a rule that if something has been stated twice, no one should say it aloud a third time.
I understand getting clarity, which makes sense, but some people talk just to hear themselves speak. So, I would sit in the meeting,

and observe the people around me. Ironically, people speak more loudly and say more with body language than when with words.

For instance, growing up I thought my mother had the eyes of an eagle and the ears of an elephant that could hear eight miles. However, once I grew up, she revealed her secrets. She explained that she had eyes and ears all over Darby Township. Without my ever realizing it, she knew my every move. My mother knew how to use her self-appointed "neighborhood watch" friends effectively for monitoring her children's social activities and watch our actions when we returned home. She would be prepared to sit and listen to my story of my adventures, then compare it to the reports from her friends. She knew that at some point in time, something in my story—if it wasn't accurate—would break down, and I would leak true information when my guard was down. She listened but she also carefully watch my body language during our conversation and when I got relaxed around the house. Her observations provided more insight into my activities then I would ever share openly.

Ironically, I have found this works with people in many roles and situations. If I sit, listen, and watch long enough, truth and motives will surface. At that point, I will know the true values behind a suggestion or plan, and to what extent I can trust the person speaking to be accountable for their actions. Being responsible for actions means understanding the consequences of my actions and sensitive to the impact on others.

We spend lots of time talking about the Millennial generation and presenting many things Millennials value or treads they have created, supported, or repurposed as if they are new. But truly nothing is new under the sun. Indeed some things are new, but many Millennial-ascribed trends are old situations dressed up in new clothing. We have a financial crisis today, but this certainly is not an unknown situation. Each generation has a group that feels they can beat the market or devise some unique financial scheme to get ahead. Problems with the stock market occurred way back in 1907 – so volatility is not new. Young people struggling to find identity or purpose has been a consistent theme with each generation, and the adults responsible for or interacting with those young people thinking the young folks have lost their way is also a story as old as time. And, despite this each generation seems to get things worked out and find the yellow brick road to success. If an individual doesn't have experience, then things will appear entirely new, but when someone with expertise takes a glance, they will step back and recognize the problem. The challenge is that you can't always rely on old methods to fix these problems but may need to implement new technologies which is why we need a workforce that is multi-generational and diverse in experience sharing ideas and solving problems.

I believe business consists of three primary parts: people, money, and resources. Remember, nothing is new under the sun. If an organization misunderstands or mismanages any of these three, success will elude, and if the three are not adequately balanced, success will be difficult.

Generation to generation individuals or groups will try to remove, mismanage, or manipulate these parts in unique manners. Within the workforce, we need to understand how to manage, develop, and encourage one another, but we can't reproduce the powerful, unique being of humankind. "Money" is what our culture trades, whether its cows, chickens, or grain or gold, land, or hard currency. "Money" is something we value and are willing to exchange for a product or service, and this will remain the same. Resources are everything else used to support, increase, or house the process of making money. Just as these things continue to stay consistent, accountability and good values will always play pertinent roles in how we interact with each other in the workplace and beyond. Responsibility and values go hand-and-hand for watching and keeping an organization aligned on a designated path. Therefore, think about this the next time someone is sitting across the desk looking for a promotion, looking for employment, or looking to do business: what are the values that drive their character? What drives their actions when they are under pressure? What are the values that drive the way they think, and will these values drive them to meet the level of accountability essential for performing the job they want well?

My boss could walk up to me tomorrow and say, "Denise, I am holding you accountable to be in Chicago tomorrow and deliver a presentation to a key client." If I do not take ownership and understand the value of this request or care about the consequences, the impact could be detrimental to the company and relationship to the client. As an employee, I may get fired if I perform poorly or contrary to the organization's values or standards. However, the cost to the company, their reputation, the client, and other staff may be far greater. The actions of one employee or group of employees are important to everyone in the organization. Remember values drive character, character drives actions, and actions determine success or failure.

[1] Seppanen, S.S., and W. Gualtieri. National Chamber Foundation. 2012. *The Millennial Generation Research Review.*
[3] Deloitte 2016 Millennial Survey. *Winning over the next Generation of Leaders.*
[7] Jansen Media Studio; Director: Mark Bussler. 2009. *Westinghouse: The Life & Times of an American Icon.* Amazon

OPINION 7

Learning the Art of Shut Up

My grandmother used to say, "Better to keep your mouth shut and be thought a fool than talk and it be proven." Her insight caused me to think twice before speaking. I wish organizations would make this simple truth a rule at meetings. Meetings would be shorter and less frequent. There is no unwritten rule that people are paid by the number of words they speak. I have sat through many two-hour or three-hour meetings only to come away thinking that the topic could have been covered in an email. Previous generations were taught only key people should speak at meetings, and each generation since has tried its best to counteract these thoughts; teaching, instead, that talking during meetings is vital in order to show how much a person knows and to stand out from the crowd.

The philosophy that high performers speak and low performers are silent at meetings undermines making sure value is being added to a conversation by what a person says. Consequently, workers are taught to rate the value of someone's work by how much a person speaks. With the birth of social media, people have become accustomed to communicating with 140 characters or less. The messages, never delivered in person, have created an unhealthy means of communication by reducing the amount of face-to-face interaction. Social media habits are influencing a very interesting dynamic in today's workplace. Two people can be in an office holding a conversation, but not actually *having* a conversation. Each person's thoughts and ideas are not connecting with the other party to the "conversation" because neither is actually listening to the other nor taking into consideration the content or purpose of the other's position. Perhaps it is because we have forgotten that conversation is more than the words but a summation of the interaction between two people has been lost. Conversation includes the words spoken, yes, but it also includes tone used, listening, and body language. We are created to influence one another, to comingle talents, and to learn from one another. Therefore, how we hold a conversation is based on how we interact with one another.

During my professional career, some of my hardest years were working as a pharmaceutical sales representative; these years were also the very rewarding because I learned a lot about how to interact with different people, how to read body language and how to manage my own tone and body language. Additionally, I was blessed with a few great mentors who taught me how to listen and serve my customers, how to be present in the moment and listen to customers' needs and problems, and how to help resolve problems. Learning to use these skills resulted in my developing a positive relationship with the doctors and their staff members, who would invite me into their office for a one-on-one conversation. Those intimate conversations taught me even more great lessons.

Before moving to the sales division of this pharmaceutical company, I was an accountant in the finance department of a large Pharmaceutical company after leaving Public Accounting where I worked for several years. Back in those days, I viewed things in black and white. I did not trust very many people. I was shy. I mumbled at times, especially when I felt tired. I avoided conflicts like the plague, and I didn't like the idea of rejection or someone yelling at me. For reasons that I cannot explain, I ventured into sales as a pharmaceutical representative for a national pharmaceutical company. Sales challenged my insecurities and tested my character. In retrospect, pharmaceutical sales helped build my character.

After spending five years as a pharmaceutical sales representative, holding one of the top territories in the nation, I walked away with a few sales awards. Yet, the best rewards were the good relationships with many of my customers. Ironically, it was not my ability to sell a product that won my customers' affection. My natural instinct to focus attention on building relationships won their devotion. I became a part of their lives. My focus on helping them solve problems had a positive influence on how we interacted. In essence, I learned to be quiet, listen, and watch.

On another occasion, one of my client offices had posted a sign on the office door saying that they didn't want to see any more sales reps that day. But when one of the nurses saw me, she immediately welcomed me in, saying "Oh, that's not for you. You're family." On another occasion, I dropped by a physician's office with a hard-to-see doctor. Just as I stepped into the office, the nurse came toward me and said that they had been waiting for me to stop by the office. They asked if I could speak with one of their patients regarding the circumstances that lead to stroke. It seemed one of their patients was nervous about the current diagnosis of stroke and changes to her lifestyle. Since I had experience and understanding about this area as a representative they thought it would be helpful for this patient to hear from someone outside the office. After a few minutes of speaking with his patient and her granddaughter, having restored her confidence, she decided to follow her doctor's advice. What his patient needed and what I provided was sincerity in my voice. Not that the physician and nurse lacked sincerity. Listening is all that is necessary sometimes to show you care. Instead of trying to sell a drug to a physician, I chose, often, to help the office solve a problem, and this resulted in the office staff trusting me. Had I not taken the time to address my customers' needs, the experience of being a pharmaceutical representative would have been completely different.

Overall, tone, body language, and the words are all part of any conversation whether you realize it or not. If you do not stay mindful of actions, you will run into problems of being misunderstood. Granted I do not always hit the mark on the nose. In fact, I am sure there are a number of people who would be happy to confirm that I have days when I have missed the mark by miles. But I have a habit of replaying conversations repeatedly in my mind that have not gone well in order to make improvements in the future. Being mindful of my actions and tone and taking note of my shortcomings has always helped me prepare for the next day.

On one occasion my actions were put to the test during a conference call with a less experienced staff member who raised his voice because he was unable to hear me speak clearly. (He also had an irritating habit of blurting out, "What!" with all of the attitude and force of a bully.) I admit that it is a struggle to suppress the urge to smack someone who speaks like that or to respond in a similar tone, but as I felt the hairs go up on the back of my neck and a slight twitch in my arm, I forced myself to stay calm. Despite the feeling of being disrespected that began to creep over me, I reminded myself that I was an experienced and knowledgeable manager. The manner in which he spoke to me challenged or questioned my abilities and values, and my reaction was not to allow the initial purpose of the conversation to be subverted to my feelings of being disrespected and undervalued.

At first, when this happened, I would not respond. I figured this team member just did not realize his actions and that perhaps, he was having a bad day. After the situation occurred a few more times, I took a pause to check my tone and decided to bring it to his attention. He was completely clueless as to the effect his responses were having on me and how they were undermining our conversations. Since then I have found that making it a habit of taking a deep breath in the face of a potential confrontation is extremely helpful for keeping mindful of my tone when responding. This practice helps me avoid workplace fire drills and drama. In the end, we were able to resolve our differences and move forward professionally.

Experienced employees in the workplace today may feel a bit uncomfortable. At the beginning of a career, an individual only sees progress up the success ladder, but usually doesn't factor in disruptions or derailment from that path. Consequently, hitting a snag on that ladder may spark a period of doubt about ability to perform or to bring value to the table. Although it is not intentional, anything that tries to reinforce this type of thinking can become a threat and possibly a tiny piece of kindling for a workplace fire. A good conversation hinges on two things: honor and respect; rank is irrelevant. If a person walks away from an interaction feeling they have been treated with honor and respect, I can almost guarantee the conversation will have been productive.

Allow me to digress to talk about the term "hierarchy" and how the perception of hierarchy and its impact on the workplace, especially in the area of a conversation, has changed. "Hierarchy" is defined as "a system in which people or things are placed in a series of levels with different importance and status." As I read this definition and think back over my career, I ponder its impact on my actions especially around conversations with members of leadership. I never took hierarchy to mean I could not have input into the decisions or have a voice with most of the people in leadership roles. I took it to mean that anyone in upper management held more of responsibility for the outcomes of the organization than I did. Yes, we all held some responsibility, but their roles and titles seemed to indicate that a greater amount of weight and expectations were placed on them. My leaders were accountable for their decisions and actions, yes, but they were also responsible for my decisions and actions. In other words, when stuff rolled down the hill it hit them first. Consequently, when we were in meetings, I tried to be mindful and consider the consequences of anything I said, knowing that they would likely carry the weight of its impact.

Today, there is a perception that hierarchy is an obsolete—and perhaps offensive—idea, and everyone should be able to speak and say anything at any time during a meeting. There should no longer be any ranking; everyone should be at the same level or be treated as if each person is at the same level.[1] My problem with this concept has to do with accountability. People want their opinions to be heard, but they do not want to be held responsible when things go wrong, either with their initial opinion or idea or with a poor outcome from their idea or plan. They also want to talk from a position of little information and virtually no wisdom. This is alarming because people like this have a tendency to ignite volatile issues and problems through untested or poorly thought-through plans. They do not have an understanding of the impact their words have on current circumstances because they lack the experience to understand how to read signs of a situation or how a chain of events might work.

However, usually having all necessary team members present at a meeting is helpful, both initially and as a follow up. I find it interesting during the recap of a meeting to gather information from the group on the main takeaways and identify any upcoming issues or risks. This practice serves to help everyone who was present to understand the bigger picture and show how decisions intertwine and keep everyone aligned. I will say there are times these conversations can be very challenging, and a lot of energy is spent knocking down walls and barriers of ego. As a leader, I don't always have the answers to questions or challenges, nor do I necessarily make the correct decisions. As a team, we help one another learn and grow. No one person ever gets to a point in his or her career when they stop growing or learning. Being willing to have an open and honest conversation allows everyone to walk away better for having had the conversation.

Nothing is better than having a real down to earth and transparent conversation in the workplace. I mean a group of coworkers and leadership sitting in a room having an honest heart-to-heart conversation about real issues, which is a productive discussion about necessary actions and defined steps needed to resolve problems. Too often management will reach out and bring in a gang of consultants, who display a fifty-page PowerPoint presentation to explain the problem, which everyone already knows is present. I am not against consultants, by any means. I happen to be one. However, most organizations do not need someone alien to the company to hop on a plane, sit in the fancy conference room, and say "Houston we have a problem." "Houston" is probably well aware of a problem.

Real conversations with real people that lead to real solutions are the answer to organizational challenges. Do not hire a company based on the reputation of their name. Look to hire individuals who bring the level of conversation and trust that will solve problems. Company name and success as a whole are irrelevant. What matters most is the person sitting across from you with their sleeves rolled up ready to architect a solution to the problem. Can you trust them enough to open your heart, comfortable enough to be transparent when sharing issues? Can you trust them to bring their experience and customized solutions, yet listen to the unique concerns of your business issues, and derive answers in partnership with your organization, versus handing over templates?

People speak, but they don't always speak anything meaningful, lots of information, but very little wisdom. Attempting to be politically correct to the point real truth is hidden, lots of ideas, but no solutions, lots of talking but no real conversations. Real conversations occur when two or more people are gathered with the agenda to talk, listen, hear, see, understand, and collaborate. The conversation should be a culmination of what is heard, seen, and understood and the real solutions developed as a result. People should learn to shut up and practice the art of listening to all sides of the table. Sometimes clients walk into meeting rooms thinking they have all the answers and want to ignore anything anyone else puts on the table; this gap needs to be waded through and bridged. On the other hand, sometimes consultants and specialists believe they have all the answers and want to ignore everyone else's ideas and serve only their own egos. Their only desire is holding up the victory flag in celebration of their individual accomplishments.

A recently coined term has emerged in lingo that gives the illusion of working together and holding meaningful conversations when in reality, in many cases, no one has any intention of doing so. This term is "partnering." Being a partner and working together to solve the problems facing business today is truly a challenge. I see the term "partnering" applied more often in the situation where one party wants to deliver all the ideas and the other party wants to sit back and be told how to fix their problem. What a combination: one party gets to be boss, and the other party gets to blame someone else when things do not work out; either way very little ownership of the final solution exists for both parties involved.

When we don't understand when to listen, when to speak, and how we all need to work together problems will not get solved and the impacts and devastations will be immeasurable. Since we hit the new millennium, we have had historical financial and business issues that have changed or affected our business culture in ways no one could have ever expected or planned for. Who knew a plane would be used as a bomb on American soil impacting the financial sector, shortly after there would be a dot.com issue, followed by the housing bubble and large (mega) powerful corporations needing to be bailed out by the government?

No one has all the answers. Cooperation, collaboration, and real conversation at the meeting table, including being quiet so that actual listening can happen is essential. Do not come to the table assuming you have the answers. A more productive strategy is to come to the table prepared to listen and work together.

As a business consultant, I tend to get challenged because I will not pretend to have a solution to impress my clients. Over the years it has become clear to me that neither client nor project team completely understands any problem. Admitting that I do not know the answer immediately takes a lot of courage. Stepping back to allow others to step forward or to sit together and design a solution requires confidence. Previous practices seem to have been to toss things up against the wall to see what might stick or to use impressive terms and pretty graphs to appear as though we have resolved the problem. However, when anyone starts peeling back the onion, a number of things become clear: misunderstandings happen. One fairly common misunderstanding is when the right people simply were not even in the room during the initial solution planning, so key elements were missed or misinterpreted.

A long time ago, I learned that a great leader knows when to lead and when to follow. I may have stated it before, but have found the serenity prayer helpful: "Lord, help me to know the things I do know, help me to know the things I do not know and have the common sense to know the difference." A wise person knows when it is time to keep their mouth shut. Learn to listen and be open to others who may shed unexpected light on the dilemma. This other person could possibly be the receptionist, the security guard at the front door, or even your dear mother who has no clue about anything relating to business, or this person could be a member of another generation. God has a sense of humor and will humble us. Remember we need one another because no one has all the answers to solve the business problems organizations face today. Learning the art of practicing silence should be a primary strategy.

[1] Seppanen, S.S., and W. Gualtieri. National Chamber Foundation. 2012 *The Millennial Generation Research Review*.

A PERSONAL NOTE

Some clarity on the themes covered in this book include:

I am not saying: All members of leadership should be from one particular generation.

What I am saying: We need skilled and experienced people at all levels of an organization, and neither age nor generation matter. Anyone with the experience to solve the problem and ability to lead a team should have the opportunity to lead regardless of age. In fact sometimes it's not even the experience but the heart of the person in leadership that makes them great.

I am not saying: This Millennial Generation is full of problems and issues making them difficult people to work under and follow.

What I am saying: Not everyone steps into a leadership role fully equipped and ready to handle all the situations, with the ability to manage people, regardless of their age or years of experience, so train those placed in leadership roles to build up their skills. Before promoting an individual, first ensure they have a firm foundation upon which skills can be built. The right heart and good motives should be the strong foundation upon which an organization builds in order to empower its leaders.

REFERENCES

1. Seppanen, S.S., and W. Gualtieri. National Chamber Foundation. 2012. *The Millennial Generation Research Review.*

2. Pew Research Center. March 7, 2014. *Millennials in Adulthood, Detached from Institutions, Networked with Friends.*

3. Deloitte 2016 Millennial Survey. *Winning over the next Generation of Leaders.*

4. World Economic Forum Report. (2016. *Future of Jobs.*

5. Patten, E., and R. Fry. March 19, 2015. Pew Report *How Millennials today compare with their grandparents 50 years ago.*

6. Derbeken, Jaxon Van. SF Gate news October 25, 2015. *Fears of failure grow for rods on Bay Bridge eastern span.*

Accessed at http://www.sfgate.com/bayarea/article/Fears-of-failure-grow-for-rods-on-Bay-Bridge-6588743.php.

7. Jansen Media Studio; Director: Mark Bussler. 2009. Westinghouse movie on Amazon

8. Grant, Ulysses S. 1885. *Personal Memories of U.S. Grant.* Charles L Webster & Co (New York). eBook published by Project Gutenberg.

www.ingramcontent.com/pod-product-compliance
Lightning Source LLC
Chambersburg PA
CBHW020924180526
45163CB00007B/2868